Content Marketing

B. Vincent

Published by RWG Publishing, 2021.

While every precaution has been taken in the preparation of this book, the publisher assumes no responsibility for errors or omissions, or for damages resulting from the use of the information contained herein.

CONTENT MARKETING

First edition. June 11, 2021.

Also by B. Vincent

Affiliate Marketing
Affiliate Marketing

Standalone
Affiliate Recruiting
Business Layoffs & Firings
Business and Entrepreneur Guide
Business Remote Workforce
Career Transition
Project Management
Precision Targeting
Professional Development
Strategic Planning
Content Marketing
Imminent List Building

Table of Contents

Content Marketing

Hello, and welcome to this course on **Content Marketing**. In this course, we'll show you how to expand your reach with the power of content. This course is divided into three modules. *Module 1* will give you a brief overview of content marketing, *Module 2*, we'll cover some content marketing tips, tactics and strategies, and *Module 3* goes over useful content marketing tools. By the time this course is over, you'll know how to leverage content marketing to bring more customers into your business. So, without further ado, let's dive into the first module. Okay guys, welcome to Module 1, in this module, our trainer will give you a brief overview of content marketing. So, get ready to take some notes and let's jump right in

Module 1

O ver the last few decades, technology has greatly evolved and will continue to do so for the years to come, and this notably changes the way people approach things, including marketing. From the birth of the worldwide web in 1989, companies have gradually transitioned to the internet to reach a bigger demographic. Now, with over 4.8 billion people using the internet every day, it's no surprise that online marketing is the king of today's advertising. The most popular type of online marketing is content marketing. Content marketing is designed to stimulate the interest of individuals by creating and sharing media to promote products or services. Major forms of content marketing include infographics, blogs, social media posts, and lead magnets. If you want to learn more about content marketing and use it to your advantage, this is the guide for you. Module 1 focuses on the benefits of content marketing and why you should use it. In Module 2, we will give you the best tips and strategies to create an effective content marketing strategy. Finally, in Module 3, we will enumerate the best content marketing tools that you can use. By the time you finish this course, you're ready to unleash the power of content marketing in your business.

According to a HubSpot survey in 2020, 70% of marketers are actively investing in content marketing, 24% of marketers plan on increasing their investments in such a strategy. When asked the value of content marketing in their business, 40% marked it as very important. What are the other latest statistics about content marketing? 94% of marketers use social media for sharing content, 91% of B2B marketers use content marketing. Videos have become the most commonly used format, 87% of video marketers say that videos have increased traffic to their website, 89% of content marketers use blog posts in their content strategy. 84% of marketers say that using infographics is highly effective. These statistics speak for themselves. If you're still relying on traditional marketing, such as magazine ads, TV commercials, or cold calling, then you're definitely missing out. In this day and age where everything is fast-paced and efficient, you want to make sure that your marketing strategy is keeping up as well. Why should you use content marketing? What are the benefits of using the strategy? Here are the top three reasons. *Builds brand awareness*- if you're new to the industry, building brand awareness is most definitely your biggest challenge. On the other hand, if you just released a new line of products or a new type of service, getting people to try it, can be a real struggle. This is where content marketing enters the picture, by creating and sharing relevant content that appeals to your target market. You can generate fresh practical topics that are in line with their problems. When you convince them that purchasing your product or service can help them solve their problems, you'll be able to upsell more products and services while building trust and establishing your brand identity.

Increase site traffic by providing valuable well-researched content to your target market. You'll gain a reputation of being a website with credible and up-to-date information. When you create helpful share-worthy content, more and more people will spread the word through their social media. This helps you to reach a wider demographic and get more people visiting your site without spending more on paid marketing. Additionally, having credible information such as blog posts help you implement a guest blogging strategy. Guest blogging, also known as guest posting, basically means writing content such as blog posts for another company's website. Guest blogging creates backlinks on different sites, which in turn boosts your brand authority and improves your organic traffic. This is very helpful for your SEO strategy. Moreover, having more site visitors means that you'll be exposed to a whole new audience that might turn to new prospects. Drives direct conversions, this is pretty straightforward. When your target market is fully convinced with your product or services, they can become potential leads. Conversions can be seen through sign-ups, account creations, downloads, form submissions, and of course, creating a sale. Transforming your site to contain compelling headlines, striking copies, eye- catchy images, and clear CTA buttons are essential to generate more conversions

Module 2

Hey folks, welcome to Module 2. In this module, our trainer will cover some content marketing tips, tactics, and strategies, so get ready to take some notes and let's jump right in.

DESPITE THE OBVIOUS reasons to use content marketing, some businesses still have a hard time implementing it simply because they don't know what to do. In fact, according to the Content Marketing Institute, 63% of businesses don't have a documented content strategy. On the other hand, some businesses have a hard time making it a reliable strategy. For instance, 65% find it challenging to produce engaging content, while 60% find it hard to consistently create content. If you're currently struggling to make your content strategy work, here are a few tips and tactics that you can use to step up your game.

Set goals. Before you create a content marketing strategy, you need to have a clear idea first of how you would approach it. To create a solid strategy, ask yourself these questions. What is my product or service? Who is the target market? What are my goals? Who are the competitors in this industry? Identify your ideal customer. In other words, who is your target market? From the word target, your aim is not a random or general group of people, but a specific audience that can be your next potential buyers. These are the people that are directly relevant to the product or service you're offering, but the question is, how can you identify these specific individuals? The answer, by identifying their persona. Follow these steps to determine what your ideal buyer would be like, identify their demographic, job and buying behavior. Determine how they would interact with your content and identify the things you need to focus on to convince them to buy your product or service. Analyze your existing content to ensure that you're always producing high quality, compelling content. You need to take a look at the statistics of your current content marketing strategy, and in this way, you'll be able to know what's hot and what's not.

Identifying the type of content that produced the most traffic and content can also serve as inspiration for future material. Analyzing also involves examining the structure of your content. For example, you can analyze the main aspects of your blogs, such as the design, layout, format, nature of the content and writing tone. If you're using a website platform, you can use its built-in metrics to analyze which blogs convert the most and which ones should be revised or discarded immediately. Gaining knowledge from these insights helps you to create the necessary changes moving forward. Research competition. Every business has its competitors, however, instead of holding a grudge, you can use it to your advantage on how you can have an edge. Analyze your competitors' blogs and social media and see what types of content they produce and how well each type performs. This helps you learn about new strategies that you can adopt and the aspects you need to focus on to create a unique voice for you to stand out from the competition.

Module 3

All right, welcome to Module 3. In this module, our trainer will go over some useful content marketing tools, so get ready to take some notes and let's jump right in.

Fortunately, there are a lot of tools available that can take your content marketing strategy to the next level. By utilizing these tools, you'll be able to reach more people in your target market and drive more conversions than ever before. SEO tools, to increase organic traffic for your website and to gain a higher ranking in your search engines, you need to have a solid SEO strategy. The main aspect of having a successful SEO is by using the right keywords for your business blog. However, finding the right keywords isn't a mere guessing game, you need to have the right SEO tools for keyword research. Here are the best SEO tools you can use.

Moz Pro, Ahrefs, SEMrush, Woorank, Google keyword planner, BuzzSumo. If you want to know what kind of content is trending in your industry, you can use BuzzSumo to research what topics your competition is writing about and how they market it. You can get content insights by identifying trending topics across all social networks. You can also run analysis reports, find industry leaders, and see what they've been sharing. Cred, Cred is a social scoring platform that allows you to find influencers that can spread awareness on your brand particularly on social media. The platform measures a person's influence by analyzing Facebook and Twitter activity and rates credibility based on two criteria, influence, and outreach. Not only is this a great tool for amplifying your message, but it also helps build your own influencer status as well. A higher credit score means that you have a larger online presence, and when your online presence increases, so will your content be.

Clickfunnels, sales funnels are essential if you want to produce highly effective conversions. Clickfunnels is a marketing automation tool that guides your site's visitors into a step-by-step process that converts them to leads to actual paying customers. What makes Clickfunnels the number one choice for companies is accessibility. Being a drag and drop platform, you can create high converting sales funnel in just a few minutes. It also provides email and Facebook marketing automation, helping you generate more leads across these platforms. Canva, who knew designing could be this easy, Canva has revolutionized graphic design by being a simple drag and drop platform with user-friendly controls that allow individuals and teams to design anything from logos, social media content, documents, cards, and more. With thousands of prebuilt templates and layouts, creating infographics and visuals for your readers will be a piece of cake. Hootsuite, of course you want to be able to share consistent content across all your social handles but doing so can be so tedious. Look no further, Hootsuite will take care of it for you, it is a social media scheduling platform that helps you schedule and post content on different social media platforms in just a few clicks. It also has a built-in spellchecker to ensure that all your posts are grammatically correct.

InVideo, nowadays more and more people are preferring to watch videos rather than reading, and this is why video marketing is another strategy that businesses should focus on. InVideo is an online video editor that helps you to create professional video content for your product or service. With a massive library of media, music, and effects combined with its easy-to-use software, you can create professional HD videos in just five minutes. InVideo provides all your creation needs packed in one simple platform. A high converting content marketing strategy is one of the biggest factors to determine the growth and success of your business. Content marketing helps you to become a trusted authority to get information, allowing you to become more visible on search engines. It also creates better traction on social media, generates more leads and improves your conversions. With brand awareness, you'll be able to convert people to become brand advocates. If you haven't done any of the things discussed, now is the time. If you already have an existing strategy, apply the tips, and use the tools mentioned to elevate your approach. When you have a solid, consistent strategy, you'll create a strong brand reputation that will take your business to new heights.

Don't miss out!

Visit the website below and you can sign up to receive emails whenever B. Vincent publishes a new book. There's no charge and no obligation.

https://books2read.com/r/B-A-QWUO-UXLPB

BOOKS 2 READ

Connecting independent readers to independent writers.

Also by B. Vincent

Affiliate Marketing
Affiliate Marketing

Standalone
Affiliate Recruiting
Business Layoffs & Firings
Business and Entrepreneur Guide
Business Remote Workforce
Career Transition
Project Management
Precision Targeting
Professional Development
Strategic Planning
Content Marketing
Imminent List Building

About the Publisher

Accepting manuscripts in the most categories. We love to help people get their words available to the world.

Revival Waves of Glory focus is to provide more options to be published. We do traditional paperbacks, hardcovers, audio books and ebooks all over the world. A traditional royalty-based publisher that offers self-publishing options, Revival Waves provides a very author friendly and transparent publishing process, with President Bill Vincent involved in the full process of your book. Send us your manuscript and we will contact you as soon as possible.

Contact: Bill Vincent at rwgpublishing@yahoo.com www.rwgpublishing.com

JOHN BOWLE

Politics and Opinion
in the Nineteenth Century

AN HISTORICAL INTRODUCTION

JONATHAN CAPE
THIRTY BEDFORD SQUARE LONDON

FIRST PUBLISHED 1954
THIS PAPERBACK EDITION FIRST PUBLISHED 1963
REPRINTED 1966

Condition of Sale

*Reprinted by Lithography in Great Britain
by Jarrold & Sons Ltd, Norwich*